PRAYER IN POETRY
MORE EXPRESSIONS OF FAITH

VICKY SPYROU-ANDRIOTIS
PRAYER IN POETRY
MORE
EXPRESSIONS OF FAITH

PUBLISHED BY
VICKY SPYROU-ANDRIOTIS
CONNECTICUT, USA

Published 2009 by Vicky Spyrou-Andriotis

Printed and bound in the
United States of America
ISBN-10: 0-9821808-1-0
ISBN-13: 978-0-9821808-1-5

Prayer In Poetry – More Expressions of Faith
www.vickyandriotis.com

Cover and Book Design – Vicky Spyrou-Andriotis

Images or photography that may be used in this book:
Copyright 2008, 2009 Vicky Spyrou-Andriotis

Dedicated To our Lord and Savior, for His gifts to us are so innumerable that I can fill enough pages about them to last a lifetime.

Written for all who "seek", in the hope that they may find.

Contents

To Heal 15
Signs 16
When I Wake 17
Be Mindful 18
United 19
Living In Color 20
Savior 21
Regrets 22
Free Yourself 23
Uninspired 24
Foundation 25
Do Not Fear 26
But A Drop 27
Fortunate Ones 28
Alive 29
My Joy Is This 30
Keep In Mind 31
Glorious, Life 32
Follow Me 33
The News 34
Bless Our Children 35
Idle Hands 36
Arise 37
Jericho 38
Good 39
Cherish 40
Free Will 41
Rejoice 42
Greater Than Ourselves 43

LIMITLESS 44
STARLIGHT 45
HELP WILL COME..46
LET THERE BE LOVE 47
THERE ARE TIMES...48
CHOOSE YOUR WORDS..49
KNOWLEDGE OF YOU 50
BOASTFULNESS AND PRIDE...................................51
EFFORTLESS 52
ONLY YOU CAN JUDGE 53
WHAT CAN DESCRIBE YOU? 54
AWAKE...55
IN PEACE..56
THE GIFT THAT IT IS..57
NEW BEGINNINGS...58
LORD, HEAR MY PRAYER.....................................59
THE GREATEST MOMENTS 60
REACH UP 61
TO REMEMBER..62
THE DAY YOU MADE 63
THE BEAT OF MY HEART......................................64
LAY IT DOWN...65
TOGETHER, WE ARE 66
THIS PRAYER 67
I SHALL REMAIN 68
IN THIS DAY, I PRAY..69
GUIDE THEM SAFELY 70
THE SOLUTION..71
BLESSED ARE WE...72
I PRAY FOR YOU...73
CLARITY, PEACE, AND LOVE.................................74
DAYS WE ARE IN...75

In Your Eyes...76
Your Love...77
The Prayers Of A Child 78
Light Of Light..79
Tell Me...80
Immortal, Eternal...81
To Speak to You 82
Worry...83
In Distress 84
How Far...85
Youth...86
When I Was a Child.......................................87
Return To Me 88
There Is Forgiveness 89
Behold..90
Proudly, My Child 91
I Am But One 92
Tears 93
Possibilities..94
Motivation 95
Comfort...96
Wherever It Leads...97
Where He Needs Me 98
Messenger...99
I Will Refrain...100

"Then you will call upon Me and go and pray to Me, and I will listen to you. And you will seek Me and find Me, when you search for Me with all your heart.."

TO HEAL

To feel Your healing power
Lord, I pray
To feel the strength You give me
Surging through my very being
Feeding my soul
Moving me forward

Take from me
The thoughts, the pains
That ail me
Body
And soul

Grant peace, that it be felt deep within me
Rippling
Calmly
Giving me the clarity
The strength
To heal from within
Through faith
Through You

SIGNS

Why do you seek signs?
Is the breeze not enough?
Are the flowers
not enough?
The moon above
The sun itself?
How can you question
Such beauty?

These are the signs provided
For those who seek
But those who have seen
Live inside their peace
Through faith
Through the joy
Such things bring

The Lord is in everything
Around you
He surrounds You
Open your heart
Then you will see

WHEN I WAKE

Waking
Into
Tomorrow
My eyes search for the familiar
And I find it in You
Lord
And I am grateful
That no matter what my tomorrows bring
You
Are in each of them

You
Are the familiar
The constant
The reason
And I find that I am grateful to wake

And I am grateful for tomorrow
And I am blessed in today
And I thank You
Lord
For
Yesterday

BE MINDFUL

That I am mindful
Of the words I speak
That I consider
Their impact
Before they reach their destination
I ask

I pray
Bind my tongue so that I am unable to utter
Unable to speak
Hurtful words
Angry
Bitter ones

I pray that goodness overflows
And the forgiveness of others is abundant
In this I hope
For this I pray
So that I may always be
Worthy
Of the forgiveness
Of others

UNITED

Keep us
Together
United
Like minded
For the good of all
And all, for good
Under God
That we all follow you
Together
Hand in hand
Joyfully
Peacefully

May our differences be few
Our understanding
And patience
Plenty

Guide us to the truth and away from
deception
Grant this to all of us
For together
We are people of God

Living In Color

Alive!
So real
Surreal
Sedate
Serene
So new

I live
I breathe
In color

Astounded
Startled
So bright
Bold
So hopeful
So full of life, this world

I celebrate You
I honor You
I praise You
And for the color
In our
Lives
I thank You

SAVIOR

Your star
It shone
And we followed

Your gifts
We sensed
And we prayed

Your voice
We heard
And we listened

Your love
We feel, still
And we grow
In mind and spirit
And in number

The Savior!
"My Savior!" we proclaim
In unison
For You have united us
Saved us
And wherever your words are spoken and
believed
There we will be

REGRETS

That my life be free from regrets
I pray
For this
My choices must be
Thoughtful
My words
Chosen carefully
And my faith
Must be
In
You

The recipe is simple
The ingredients
Are few
And yet
It is this simplicity
And thoughtfulness
That will turn these elements
Into a life I will be proud
To have lived
And one
Free
From
Regrets

FREE YOURSELF

Have you freed your mind from thoughts
Disruptive
To your soul?

Have you replaced the noise that tries
To break
Your spirit
The noise that seeps into your mind from
somewhere outside
Spreading thoughts
Untrue?

Prayer can free you
Faith can free you
The Truth
Can free you

You are more than what you believe you are
More than what you've been told
For God has made you so

Free yourself from the noise
And find
The real
You

UNINSPIRED

If I am uninspired
Then my heart has betrayed me
My eyes have failed me
My fear has kept me from living today

If I am uninspired
With such blessings around me
Such love that has found me
Then I am dumbfounded
For there is no reason
No logic
No cause
For lack of motivation
Or Inspiration

The answers are around me
Invigorating
Motivating
Inspiring

I must choose to see
Listen
Accept
For if I am uninspired
The fault
Is mine
Alone

FOUNDATION

I seek
A foundation
Sturdy
Unshakable
On which to build this life I've been given

It must be made with care
And comprised of faith and love
In You
Without which, it can not stand
It will be weak
And unable to bear
The weight
Of life's joys
As well as its burdens
Faith will make it
Solid
Love will make it
Last
You
Will keep it
Strong

DO NOT FEAR

Alone
You search for your place in this life
Disenchanted
Fearful
Why do you fear?
Things will be
As they should

Time
It comes
Time
It goes
Your choices now
Determine
Where the end shall find you
No need to make them
Alone

Pray for guidance
Pray for direction
Pray for strength

And all
Will be
Right

But A Drop

To give
When your cup is full
Is kind
Indeed
And shall have its reward
That is certain

To give
When there is but a drop for you to taste
And you
Share freely
Regardless
Reveals a heart, pure, selfless, true
Rewards await you
Both here
And in
The
Ever
After

You are blessed
And worthy of all
Which you
Shall receive

FORTUNATE ONES

Fortunate ones
I count myself
Among them

Laughter
Around us
Love
Inside us
Peace
Among us
Understanding
Between us

The sun inside our souls
Shining brightly
Warmly

Fortunate
And thankful
Fortunate
We pray
Fortunate
We know
That it is all by the will of God
That we are
And remain
The fortunate ones

ALIVE

Blue skies
Pastel moons
Drops from the ocean
Flicker upon crystal sands
In the afternoon
Connected
And alive
These things to us
As we are
To each other
And with every encounter
We are reminded of our Creator
Each
Gives us greater understanding
Of our own existence
Each
Placed before us
To be cared for and appreciated
To unite us
To invite us
To feel
Alive

My Joy Is This

My joy is this
To write
For it is a gift You give to me

My joy is this
To write these words to You and for You
My mind
My heart
Are full of praise and love

Tell me, Lord
What more can I give of myself
These words are not enough
There are not enough words
What more can I do
With this gift?

A difference should be made
A difference in the world
A difference with these words
For my joy
Is to write them

KEEP IN MIND

Be grateful
Be thankful
When your worries are few
And your blessings are many
Keep in your heart and mind
Those who might need
Just
A little bit
More
Those whose worries
Exceed your own
For even when your burdens are heavy
There are still more weighty
Than yours

Be grateful
Be thankful
And reach out your hand
And thank the Lord above
That someone
has reached out
To touch
Yours

GLORIOUS, LIFE

Life
Often glorious
Sometimes tiresome
Always worth
The time we give
And the time we take
Worth all the love
And those with whom we share it
Those to whom we give it
Worth every sight
And every sound
That we create ourselves
Or that has been created for us

Our lives
Worth moving forward
Or just standing still
Turning
And often tumbling
Worth every prayer we pray
And everything we pray for
This
Our glorious
Life

FOLLOW ME

"Who do you say that I Am?"[⊕]
I Am the light
I Am the wind
I Am the earth
And the stars

I Am the key
Of which there is but One
Without Me
The Gates
Shall remain
Locked

Only those who hold Me dear
Hold Me close
Know My worth
Will have Me to open the doors
And Me to follow through them

"Who do you say that I Am?"
I Am all that is
And all that ever
Will Be
Follow Me

[⊕] The Holy Bible (NKJV™) – Matthew 16:13

THE NEWS

The angels sang and rejoiced
And shouted the news
To all who would hear

The heavens danced
The stars gleamed
One showed the way
To the place where You lay Your head
And the world was forever changed
And into it
Came
Love
Unconditional, timeless

Your love
Like You
Is everlasting
Never ending
And still we rejoice!
For on that day
You
Were born

BLESS OUR CHILDREN

Oh Lord
I pray
Bless our children
That they may remain steadfast and true
That their mistakes are few
And their successes are many
That they are compassionate
And willing
To serve
To teach
To pray

That they are forever and
Ceaselessly
Mindful of the root, the cause, the reason
For their success
For it all
Stems from You

May their gratitude show in the works they
do
And the words they say

Amen

IDLE HANDS

Idle hands
Made by idle hearts
To bring your heart to life
Your hands must work
To feed a hungry child
To ease the worries and fears of a mother
To lift her to her feet

Your brow must sweat
And your heart must burn
With the misery you've helped to ease
Only then will your heart beat
Effortlessly
Only then will it be worth
The love that it takes
And the air that it needs
Only then
Can you bring your heart
To life

ARISE

I arise
For You have touched me
I arise
For You have healed me
I arise
For You have saved me
And all my afflictions
And all the thoughts that have imprisoned
me
And those that fall like barriers around me
And serve to hinder me
Have been cast
Away from me
Flung into the ashes of their own remains

I arise
Because You command it
I arise
Because I am able
And willing
I arise
Because my faith in You
Has made it so

JERICHO

If you find me on your journey to Jericho
I pray
Do not cross the road, away from me
Won't you stop
And take my hand instead?

Won't you stop
And offer a kind word for my ears to hear
A smile for my eyes to see
A glass of water
For my thirst
A crumb from your meal
So that my belly can be full
And rejoice in its good fortune?

Choose mercy over indifference
"love your neighbor as yourself"[⊕]
Let His words fill your heart
And let His words
Be your guide

[⊕] The Holy Bible (NKJV™) – Matthew 22:39

GOOD

In good health
In good spirits
In good company
May we always be

Keep from peril
The ones we love
Keep in mind
Those who believe
Help us to pray
For those who do not

Let our hearts beat in time
Let our minds be in tune
That we might spend our time caring for
others
As God has cared for us

Amen

CHERISH

Cherish
What I have
And hold
What I honor
And love
What completes my life
What makes me whole

Cherish those
Whom God has brought to me
For me
So that I might know love
So that I might give it
And take it
Nurture it
And believe in it

Cherish them now
So that I may never know the world
Without their love
Or
His

FREE WILL

That we use our free will
Wisely
Honorably
For this I pray

That we not mistake our abilities
As if
We are entitled to use them
And I pray that we understand the difference

That our free will should not be used
Recklessly
Selfishly

That our choices take into account
The well being of others
That we use our free will to do the will
Of the Creator
Who bestowed it
Upon us
I pray

REJOICE

Rejoice!
The day is near
Rejoice!
In the miracle
Of the day He arrived
Rejoice
And let the world over
Hear the joyful sound of our voices
United
Together
In song

Rejoice!
For this is the day of immeasurable joy

Be light in it
Be glad in it
This is the day
To
Rejoice!

GREATER THAN OURSELVES

We are chosen
For tasks much greater than we know
For lives
More meaningful than we understand
For roads
That lead to places we do not know

We must take care
Not to let our choices lead us away
From the things we are meant to pursue

We must leave our lives
Our minds
Our hearts
Open to the possibilities
The opportunities
That seem to choose us, instead
So that one day
We may find that we have lived lives
Much greater
Than ourselves

LIMITLESS

The world that tells you
The possible
From the impossible
Has not felt hope
Has lost its faith
For with Him
All things are possible
All are limitless

Capable
Incapable
One is simply a boundary of the mind
And of the world
The line between which can be crossed at
any time
By a heart that has been freed
By faith

Nourish your faith
And let
Your world
Be
Limitless

STARLIGHT

There
In the starlight
There
In its glow
I feel You
Watching
Guiding

Starlight falling
To light my way
Starlight
As if from Heaven itself
So bright and pure

Starlight
To remind us
That You
Are ever present
That You
Are there to guide us
That
You
Are

HELP WILL COME

Why do you walk
This lonely mile?
Why do your shoulders
Carry such weight
Such worry
Such dismay
There is no shame
In asking for a hand to hold

Help
Is as close as a prayer
Prayer
Is as simple as a breath
A breath that sustains you
Giving you life
Filling you
Naturally
Effortlessly

Pray
Effortlessly
Naturally
Pray
So that your worry has a voice
Pray
So that your voice is heard
Pray
And help will come

46

LET THERE BE LOVE

Lord
Let there be love
Let not the actions of those to whom I
Entrust
Pieces of myself
Be the cause of my grief
My anger
My sadness
Let them, instead, bring peace to my life
And me to theirs
For there is enough grief in the world
That we should stand together
Against it, as friends
Not apart, like strangers

Let there be love
That the pieces of me be kept safely in the
hearts
Of those
I love

THERE ARE TIMES

There are times, Lord
That I wished you couldn't see me
There are times, Lord
When I instantly regret
An action
Unbecoming
A word
Cutting through air
Inflicting wounds that can not heal
And I pray
That You know my deep remorse
That You feel my sorrow
That You realize my shame

There are times
When I seek forgiveness
For only then can I return my heart
To joy
My soul to light
And my mind
To peace

CHOOSE YOUR WORDS

Friend
When words escape you
Speak none
For it is better to be silent
Than to be a "noisy gong"

Speak only words you believe
And refrain from those
That will only
Cause harm

Look to the Lord to be your guide
And imagine His reaction to your words
Should you imagine that they bring a smile
to His lips
Then surely
They are just and true
But
Should your heart be uneasy when you think
of Him
Then choose
Your words
Again

KNOWLEDGE OF YOU

Lord, my God
What words should I impart
To those who would
Deny You
To those
Full of pride
To those
Who must be saved
Whose ignorance has made
Blind?

Forgive them, Lord
And help me to inspire
And guide them
Open their hearts and minds to the truth of
Your ways
Your love
Your sacrifice

Help me to bring the passion in my heart
To my lips
And impart the knowledge of You
To those who need it the most

BOASTFULNESS AND PRIDE

Boastfulness and pride
Serve man alone
There is no satisfaction
That can be derived from it
It is only temporary

Seek the things that serve God
And find
Fulfillment
That is everlasting

Do not exalt yourselves
Or deem yourselves above others
For brothers and sisters
Are loved equally by their father
Boastfulness and pride
Will not hasten their reward

EFFORTLESS

Is not our love for each other effortless?
For what reason, Lord, is this not so?
Should not people of faith
Love willingly
Freely?

I pray that You remove this coldness
From within us
Replace it with the desire to receive another
freely
To love
Regardless of beliefs
Circumstance
Or common thread

Are we not Christians?
Then let us put to practice
What we've only learned
To say

ONLY YOU CAN JUDGE

Lord
Let their anger and judgment pass over me
It is in vain
For only You can judge what is proper and
true
And show us what is false
And detrimental to our souls

Judgment
Hurtful
Deceitful
Purposeless
Motives unknown
Unkind

I Strive to be honorable
Moral
Good
And when judgment is spoken
By those who seek vengeance
It will not
Easily
Be
Believed

WHAT CAN DESCRIBE YOU?

The best of all poems
The finest of words
Can hardly describe
Even the least of You

You are love
You are peace
Time
Space
The earth
And the sky
The clouds
And the sun

All of these
Together
And at once
All of these
One by one
All of these
And more
Though more can not be measured
Nor understood
Mere words
Simply fail
To describe
You

AWAKE

It is not a dream
Nor am I asleep
When I feel that You are near
I've but to look about at all that I am
And all that I have
To know
That I am
Awake

Both body and soul, awake
I do not stumble through each day
Unaware
I do not close my eyes and hope to dream of
the things I desire
For because of You
I am blessed with them inside my waking
hours

I have not dreamt You
Not imagined You
I am awake
And know
That You are near

IN PEACE

Peace
A state of being
A place to live in
Not imprisoned in a thought
Or an idea
But released into the world

It was created
For it was intended to be
I pray for our strength to resist all that is
contrary

For a world
Ensconced in peace
Can not perish
Will not wither
Can not die

It can only flourish
And thrive
And so
Shall we

THE GIFT THAT IT IS

The day
It unfolds
Unwrapping, slowly
Like the gift that it is
It pushes forward
Full of promise

From the hours
To the minutes
To the moments
That I am
I thank and praise You

For the days
And the weeks
That fill my years with joy and hope
I praise You and I pray
That they reveal themselves
Slowly
As I patiently
And joyfully
Await for each new day to unwrap
Like the gift that it is

NEW BEGINNINGS

Lord
These thorns, they hinder me
Preventing me from moving forward
I pray
Remove them from my side
And I will not take for granted my good
fortune and health
I will not forget to be grateful for the
absence of their ache
I will keep them near to me always

Each time I persevere or overcome
I will remember to be glad
I will remember the times I stood still
And be joyful
And purposeful
As I find myself moving
Toward
New beginnings

LORD, HEAR MY PRAYER

Lord, hear my prayer
For I am frightened
And seek comfort
So much I've left to give
So much I've yet to find
To share
To be
For myself and for others
For You

Keep my body free from harm so that I may
continue to use it
To work tirelessly for the good of the world
around me
For the family that nurtures me
For the eyes that have met mine
And for those I've yet to see
Keep me safe
Keep me strong

Lord, hear my prayer

THE GREATEST MOMENTS

You smile down upon our victories
Rejoice in our triumphs
And gently guide us to them
We invoke Your name
Seeking help
Relief
Strength
Or courage

These things
And more
You provide to all who believe

Both Father and Son
We seek You
And find You
In our victories
In our triumphs
And through our prayers
For You
Are in all the greatest moments
Of our lives

REACH UP

Fearful
Sorrowful
Within yourself
You search for light inside the darkness

Reach up!
Reach out!
That God might answer your call for
comfort
Through the presence of a friend
Through the words of a loved one
Through the kindness of a stranger
In the smile of a child
In the places you seek
And in places, unexpected

You've but to call
And know He'll send your answer
You've but to reach
And know that He will place it
Within
Your grasp

TO REMEMBER

Such treasures You make
As in this child
So pure and free
So like the breeze
So like the color of a rainbow
So clear, the mind
And pure, the heart
Remarkable to witness, and a lesson to be
learned
For all to remember
How to be as pure
And free
To remember
The treasure that they were
And the treasure they've become
As in this child

For You
Have made
Us all

THE DAY YOU MADE

Lord
For the ability to accomplish my goals today
I thank You
For removing any obstacles
Or helping me to avoid them
I thank You
For allowing me to step forward
Without fear of falling back
I thank You
For putting those I love
Somewhere inside my day
I thank You

This is a day
That You have made
And I am thankful
To be
In it

THE BEAT OF MY HEART

There rises before me
Your glorious sun
Rising to meet the sky
Rising to greet the day
It warms my body
And inspires my soul
Lifting my spirits

There I hear my beating heart
As much a miracle
As the sun itself
I count the beats while the
Sun makes its entrance into my day
And I am filled with warmth
And wonder
And I am filled with gratitude
And peace
Knowing that You
Are the reason
That the sun rises
To the beat of my heart

LAY IT DOWN

Lay down your sadness
Lay down your burdens
Lay down the darkness
That you hide inside you
And be lifted
To a place
Indescribable

Do not be bound by fear
Do not be led by your pain
Do not be held to your past
Release them
Allow them to flow out from within you
Be free of the darkness
And be led by your faith instead
Only then will you find
The life that you seek
It is only when you walk in the light
And leave behind the shadows
That you
Can be
Lifted

TOGETHER, WE ARE

Together
Bound together by our common hopes
Together
We stand together
Brought here
By God
By our faith in Him
And in each other
Together
I am awed at the power of our faith and our
love combined

The earth trembles with the sound of our
voices
United
Joyful
The earth trembles
For it can not contain
The boom of our laughter
The force of our hope
The strength of our will to bring peace
And unity
To our world
The earth trembles
For we are
Together

THIS PRAYER

In this I find contentment
Peace
This prayer brings me serenity
These thoughts from me to You
In this moment
I lack for nothing
I ask for nothing
I am only compelled to think of You
There are no things I desire
Only to imagine Your presence
To feel it
For a moment
To feel warmth
Calmness
Contentment
Knowing You are here
And everywhere
I send You
My love

I SHALL REMAIN

I am
And will be
I am
And shall remain
Faithful to what I believe
For of that I am sure
And know to be true
When all else fails
When the world is unpredictable
God remains
Constant
Ready
Present
Of this I can be sure
And so I am
And will be
And shall remain
Faithful
To what I believe
Always

IN THIS DAY, I PRAY

In this day
I pray, surround me
With the love of a friend
With a word of encouragement
With a warm embrace
And a random kindness

In this day
I pray, that all is right with the world
That our challenges do not exceed our
abilities
That the weight of our worries does not
exceed
The strength of the shoulders on which they
are carried
That a goal
Is always in sight
While another
Is achieved
That our faith in God
Ourselves
And in humanity
Is enough to see us through any day
But our friends remain beside us
Anyway

GUIDE THEM SAFELY

Oh
What sadness
For the needs of the world are not met
The fault of those
Who take more
Than they give
Those who have left their brothers in despair
They are of no concern to me
For they shall be accountable by One much
greater than us

But Lord
Let Your light shine upon those who feel
hopeless
Have lost themselves in their despair
Their direction is not clear
And Your light will guide them
Safely
Back to where
They
Belong

THE SOLUTION

Can we breathe
In the midst of this
Uncertainty
In this cloud
That takes our breath away
In these times
So troubled, so broken

You are our lifeline
The very air we need
The air we breathe
In this troubled world
We can find new life
Through You
You are our salvation
Our reason
Our inspiration
And our answer

You are in each and every life sustaining
breath that we take
You are the air itself
You are
The solution

BLESSED ARE WE

Blessed are we
Who in our fear
In our anxiety
Our prayers are heard and help arrives
Our minds are eased
And we begin to heal

Blessed are we
Who turn to You when fear creeps in
Who think of You
Before all else
Our faith rewarded
Our lives to mend

Blessed indeed
And thankful

Blessed are we
Who
Believe

I PRAY FOR YOU

Precious angels
I pray for your joy
And your health

I pray for your
Blessing from above
That you are looked upon with favor
That you remain as precious in His eyes
As you are in mine

I pray that wherever you walk, happiness
follows
Wherever you stand, joy rains down upon
you
That wherever you lay your heads, warmth,
peace, and comfort surround you

I pray that your faith
Grows
As you do
I pray
For you

CLARITY, PEACE, AND LOVE

Clarity
Peace, love
All unfold
In time

What you seek
Is easily found
Clarity achieved
Body and soul
Through conversations with God

Listen
Follow
See through your mind's eye what your eyes
are afraid to see

See patiently
See thoughtfully
Faithfully
And clarity
Peace
And love
Will find you
Body
And
Soul

DAYS WE ARE IN

Better days will find us
Although
Even in these
We are blessed
Even as we struggle and look forward to the
days to come
There is much to be grateful for
Today

Better days will come
Patience and prayer
Persistence
And hope
Purpose
And trust
That better days will find us
Will help us emerge
From the days
We
Are
In

IN YOUR EYES

How do you see me, Lord?
In your eyes
Am I worthy of the things I possess?
How do I become more pleasing
To You
How will I know that I am?

That my works speak for themselves
I pray
That a change will come
That a change will stay

To be worthy in Your eyes
Is the greatest task I can hope to complete
In this life
And in the next
And will strive
In all that I do
To be worthy
In Your Eyes

YOUR LOVE

Is there a limit to Your love?
There is not, of this I'm sure
Is there no measure?
There is not
It can not be contained
Nor explained
No description can be written
No imagination
Can conceive
The depth
The height
The magnitude
Even the existence
Of such a love
And yet
It is because of it
That we live
And breathe
That we came to be
And are
Still
And yet, we can not fathom the immensity
The intensity
Of Your Love

THE PRAYERS OF A CHILD

Oh Lord
Hear the prayers of a child
Who with faith asks for nothing more
Than health
To feel
Like others feel
To do
As others do
To live
As others live

Hear the prayers of a child
Your beloved and chosen
Your most faithful
And innocent
Your most deserving of all Your creations
Of all who follow You

A child who prays does not question
Does not wonder
But only believes in You
And for this I ask
Oh Lord
Hear the prayers of a child

LIGHT OF LIGHT

Light of Light
Ray of hope
Radiant
Brilliant
And blinding
Your promise
Your goodness
Illuminate the way
And lead us to roads
Unseen before Your light shown down upon
them

The hope of You
Disperses shadows and darkness
They are no more
No longer do we hide behind them
Beneath them
For we are now
Sheltered
By the Light

TELL ME

Talk to me
Take my hand
Let me know
That I walk in the right direction
That I think as I should
Love as I should
Live as I should
Give
As I should

Tell me
So that I might find my name written in the
book
When time
Has run its course and is no more
So that I might be counted among those who
have served
Those who have
Given
And those
Who have
Loved

IMMORTAL, ETERNAL

Your arms
Extended
Your clothes
Tattered
Your eyes
Speak of sorrow
They are as troubled as a storm

Forgiving
Hopeful
You lift your head
And whisper towards the sky
Your words
Drift and linger
And echo into the hearts and souls of all
who love
All who believe

A final breath
Your spirit released
With the grace of a dove, You fly
Off to the place You belonged
Eternal
Immortal
Your wounds have healed
And so have ours

TO SPEAK TO YOU

It is difficult to speak at times
To speak to You
Uncertain
What to say

And so I begin with expressions of gratitude
For all that is
And all that will be

Then
There is my love for You
Ever present
Constant
This I must convey as well

I must tell You of all who are dear to me
And ask that you guide
And protect them

These things I say
These things I pray
And find that they
Are not
So difficult
After all

WORRY

Worry
Can not bring change
Worry
Fractures hope
Fuels fears
Distracts
From the joy of living
From the joy in now

Worry
Contradicts your faith

Quiet your fear
And bclicvc in what you pray
That all can be conquered through Him
All can be found
And all can be saved

Cast your worries aside
And live
Today

In Distress

Lord
I beseech you to resolve
That which distresses me so
Let it pass quickly
Its impact
Minute

My heart is heavy
As I wonder
And I ponder
The how
And the why

Let these unimportant things that dwell in
my thoughts
Fade quickly
And give way to those
Of
You
The mercy You show
The love You give
And the comfort
You bring

HOW FAR

The Earth we know
The stars
How far beneath You
How far beneath Your gates do we travel?

I pray our intentions are closer that we
That our works bring us a step closer to
heaven

I pray that we are near
But that the gift of time is granted
That our earthly life
Shall be full
And joyous
Honorable
I pray that we walk near to you
And when we are no longer bound by time
I pray the gates
Open
Effortlessly

YOUTH

Oh youth
You are but a tool
We use
Often unwisely
Foolishly we seek
Things of little significance
And carelessly endanger
Our souls and bodies

Youth
You blind us to the truth
And often keep us from
The path
That leads us to our true
Reward

You are a gift
To be used
Wisely and with great care
So that when you are gone
Wisdom remains

WHEN I WAS A CHILD

When I was a child
I knew nothing of the material

When I was a child
It was love that fulfilled me
The company of living things
God's wonders
That inspired feelings
And ideas
That were imperishable, unlike material
treasures

When I was a child
Love was the only necessity
Indispensable requirement
To growing and thriving
Riches were not measured by the things I
possessed
But by what I could feel
The love that I gave
And the love I received
When I
Was a child

RETURN TO ME

When you have lost your way
When all you've treasured
And all you have measured
And counted
And followed
Have failed you
When the world is not as it seemed
And the gifts you possessed have been
squandered

Return to Me

To where all is forgiven, and I will rejoice
with you
For you will have understood

Return to Me

And the days of your absence will be
forgotten
Your love will be welcomed
And returned

Return to Me

And be found
Again

THERE IS FORGIVENESS

There is forgiveness
To give
To receive

There is forgiveness
For us
And from us

Such foolish things that keep us from each
other
From love
Such foolish things that bring us to anger
That cause use to lose our connection
One to another

Search not for the errors
For the reasons to love outnumber them
And as for the sins of our past
And those yet to be
There is always
Forgiveness

BEHOLD

Oh!
How blessed I am
To behold
That which
I had only dreamed of
And prayed for

To hold you in my arms
For the first time
And forever
God smiled upon me
At that moment
Through your gaze

So radiant
Unbelievable
Unforgettable
And undeniably
A God-given moment
To last
A lifetime[⊕]

[⊕] From "Prayer in Poetry For The Christian Mother".
Used By Permission. Copyright ©2008 V. Andriotis

PROUDLY, MY CHILD

Proudly
I say
You are my child
Confident and hopeful
Mighty and brave
You lift my spirits
My heart, it soars

Your courage is evident
Your compassion overflows
I pray you use
The things you are
To better the lives of all
Whom you encounter

To lift them up
To affect change

Praise and thank Him
Every day
By giving of yourself
What the Lord has given you
And know
That you are blessed$^{\oplus}$

$^{\oplus}$ From "Prayer in Poetry For The Christian Mother".
Used By Permission. Copyright ©2008 V. Andriotis

I AM BUT ONE

For I am but one
Though the voices of many find their way
higher
From where they began
Those, sent upward
Believing
Reach their destination

I am but one
Among the voices of many
The voices of mothers
The voices of daughters
From those who care
And those who are cared for
For each other
About each other

My voice is but one
My prayers are many
I pray
Believing
That they will be heard
Even though
I am
But one[⊕]

[⊕] From "Prayer in Poetry For The Christian Mother".
Used By Permission. Copyright ©2008 V. Andriotis

TEARS

Tears
Stream
From tired eyes
My joy
Has no words
My relief
Has no other expression
My faith is fortified
My love
Is multiplied
God
Shall be magnified
By all who enter here

In this home
Faithful reside
And those who know
That He walks beside us
Have crossed the threshold
And have
Found peace
Within[⊕]

[⊕] From "Prayer in Poetry For The Christian Mother".
Used By Permission. Copyright ©2008 V. Andriotis

POSSIBILITIES

Oh Lord
I pray
That this house be filled with laughter
That our lives be full of possibilities
That our love be ever growing
That our family be strong
And faithful

I pray
That God is in our actions
And in our reactions

May we continue to walk through life
Together
With grace
Attaining wisdom
Maintaining our faith
And being ever closer
To each other
And to God

Amen [✝]

[✝] From "Prayer in Poetry For The Christian Mother".
Used By Permission. Copyright ©2008 V. Andriotis

MOTIVATION

What truly drives us
Motivates us
Inspires us
Is for God, alone to know
For truly
It can not be put into words
Only what is assumed
What we see
Passes for motivation
In the eyes of others

But God knows our hearts
He knows all
He knows purity
From vanity
And knows with certainty
Which
Motivates us
The most

COMFORT

Lord
Teach me to be of comfort
To those in need
I do not ask to understand what I am not
meant to
I only ask to help ease the suffering
Of those who might find
Themselves
Hopeless
In need
In pain

Perhaps it is not for me to understand death
Or loss
But allow that I can help those who grieve
find their way back to You
Show me the way
To help them
Find their faith
And know
That in time
They will understand
Your ways

WHEREVER IT LEADS

On Your footstool, Lord
We seek to build lives worthy of You
With wisdom and purity
Granted to us
We can accomplish many things

Here we shall build
A place where You will rest Your feet
A place where Your children will grow
A place where Your faithful will pray
A place to wait
Until our journey leads us near to Your
Throne
For we are among those who hear Your
words
And follow Your voice
Wherever
It
Leads

WHERE HE NEEDS ME

The dreams I hold are many
Though what may come
Is unknown
I fear not
For I leave the future in the hands of God

I listen and watch
I pray and listen
And I ask that He lead me through my
intuition
And through my inspiration

Without doubt
I believe
That I will find myself where He
Needs me to be

MESSENGER

I pray
To be Your messenger
To spread the essence
Of
You
Far and wide
And to all who will hear
And to all who will not

Make that whatever my hands touch
And my eyes see
Understands and feels
The hope
Of You

If it is Your will
If it is my purpose
I pray
Let my mission begin

I WILL REFRAIN

Oh Lord
My foolishness follows me
My regrets haunt me
What causes such babble to bleed from my
lips
Time and again

I try to refrain
I promise to become kinder
And wise
Yet
I perceive such babble has caused
Tension and ill-will
Which can not be pleasing to You
And is not the outcome
I had intended

I ask for forgiveness
From You
And from my brothers and sisters
Whom I have offended
And promise
To try and show them
Kindness
Again

www.ingramcontent.com/pod-product-compliance
Lightning Source LLC
Chambersburg PA
CBHW031520040426
42445CB00009B/327